The Waiting Hillside

The Waiting Hillside

Martin Malone

Templar Poetry

Published in 2011 by Templar Poetry
Templar Poetry in an imprint of Delamide & Bell

Fenelon House
Kingsbridge Terrace
58 Dale Road, Matlock, Derbyshire
DE4 3NB

www.templarpoetry.co.uk

ISBN 978-1-906285-30-2

A CIP catalogue record of this book is available from the British Library

Typeset by Pliny
Graphics by Paloma Violet

Printed in India

For Joan & Alex

Acknowledgements

Acknowledgements are due to the following publications and competition anthologies, in which some of these poems first featured:

Stand, Assent, The Reader, Acumen, Orbis, Muse, About Larkin, The Hardy Society Journal, The Brontë Society website, The Binturong Review, The French Literary Review, PoetryWeb, the Mirehouse Poetry Competition 2011, Yorkshire Open Poetry Competition 2010 and *Battered Moons Poetry Competition 2010*.

Barbury Castle appeared on BBC Radio 4's 'Today Programme' homepage as part of their 'Magic of Place' feature.

Digitalis was the winner of the 2011 Wivenhoe Poetry Prize.

I'd like to thank the Wordsworth Trust for my place on their mentoring scheme and Paul Batchelor for his help in putting together this collection. I'd also like to thank Hilda Sheehan at Bluegate Books for her unwavering support and for publishing my previous pamphlets, *17 Landscapes* and *19 Paternosters*.

Contents

"Each one of us, then, should speak of his roads, his crossroads, his roadside benches; each one of us should make a surveyor's map of his lost fields and meadows."

- Gaston Bachelard

At Uffington

You stepped back a pace to better
your gaze into the low winter sun
and frame the prospect: man bends
to boy with kite and deals with a rogue
top button – a candle flame inclined
to the draught at the door of implied
fatherhood. You too fasten this moment
smiling at its easy eternity;
its archetype of family
held safe, all the same, against
the chill of our unravelling.
I'll later drive north, the tug
of necessary space pulling
me back into normal orbit.

But, for now, we stand on Dragon Hill,
our own slain myth bleeding circumstance
onto hope. Your boy persists;
circles the bare chalk patch, his arm
forty-five degrees supplicant:
Epona's child of flight and air
favoured, forsaken, lifted again.
Fertility, death and healing: chaff
for the horse goddess. The fickle line
rises. Your restive hand finds mine,
capricious in turn. Caught beyond
caution, we rejoin the moment;
driving deep the flint of it into
the chalky quick of ancient time.
Scouring out our own curt lore
under the dancing hooves of
a white horse.

Barbury Castle

Meet me at the earthworks
      in the small hours on the hill.
Up there, above your childhood,
      at the swing-door of first light
as – mouthful of stars –
      another time-laden night
does its excuse-me with the dawn.

Here, beyond the tidemark
      of Swindon's dirty ochre,
power up the heart's deep electric
      and bring to me your darkness.
Let me reach towards its livewire
      it larksong static, earth your now
in the harebells, ox eye, horseshoe vetch.

Meet me at the earthworks:
      murus gallicus, univallate,
gate-gone to cowslip, chalkhill blue,
      bolt-shot to harebell and to you.
And, to you, I too am wide open;
      under the ages' weight of starlight
and slow time; waiting for the day.

Up North Combine

Cat member of a pigeon family,
I never saw the appeal. Those scrawny
dozen concessions to Dad's first coronary.
We billeted them in the old coal-house;
my father winding down from working life
in the second childhood of friends reunited.
Ma's reluctant grant to mortality.

Home for the weekend, the throaty bubbling
took me back – thriven on my own brood
memory – to the creak of wickerwork,
rattle of corn tins, clucking of time clocks
and the lairy stink of pedigree birds.
The *Up North Combine* had lorried up to collect
and I'm walking home from my Primary.

Like old man Steptoe, he was a hoarder
my father. So no good at necking the chaff.
The hatchlings added up. He lacked the butcher's
heart of a serious racer, so spared them
one-and-all; clogging up the shed like his
own blocked aorta. My mother protested
and pleaded sense but loved his last pleasures.

Cat member of a pigeon family,
it was left to me. Low-bred beyond
adoption with an instinct for return,
just smart enough not to lose their way,
I couldn't rid them of attraction
so rid them of themselves: snapping their necks
to save my mother from remembering.

Seascape

You asked what ailed me, spotting the sudden
riddle of distress in your spooked infant.
Darkness was upon me: darkness black
and boy-shaped; riding the press of sands,
smearing the sunlight in its own sharp threat.
Father, the distance then between us spanned
but the lag of seconds whilst you worked out
my dilemma. Then you saw him too: a dark
familiar child hemming itself onto
your own distraught blood. Clearing a nimbus,
the sun quickened his outline as you smiled
and pointed to your own burden, bigger
than mine and no less dogged in pursuit.
We've all got one it seems, even Daddy.
So that's alright. Better to know. What now?
For all we ran that day, there was neither
catching nor escaping. Your shadow, long
beyond the sandbank; I am chasing it still.

Trouvé

I prise open a new year at Easter
with the big key to my green front door.

There, on the floor of the light-slatted
kitchen, a one-word note from Autumn.

Clenched in the yellow palm of dusted leaf,
your parting shot is my Spring greeting.

I throw wide the shutters, recreate the room
and stoop to pick up the twist, retrieve the script.

Nightjar

I set out at midnight, riding
the bad-land pleasure of
quiet motorways 6 and 5;
iPod aglow on the dashboard
like the embers of a campfire.

The moon is full in a star-struck sky,
as I quietly let myself in.
Picking my way through the kitchen
I hear breathing. There, prone on
the prairie of the living room floor,
your boy is camping out tonight.

I stop in the doorway at the foot
of the stairs; paused in equidistance,
between the dormant child with my
lost talent for sleep and a thrilling
climb to the waiting electricity
of your smooth, sleep-warm skin.

I come to you as shadow and breath,
roused to vague archetype; my flesh
chilled by night air and jarred hard
by want. When I join you, I am
anonymous: my lover's cipher,
decoding dark journeys of desire.

Avebury

Matchstick arm over pipe-cleaner knee,
his climbing shadow prints a sloping 'A'
in retro font upon the ditch's green.

Across the v-shaped space of 4,000 years
and one half-lived lifetime, I watch him
as a father watched my own ascensions.

There he weaves his crosswise tick of life
through sarsen stone and absence, against
the tight warp of my remoter seeing.

Climbing with purpose, this something-to-me
child of another man pauses and turns
to wave at me, blinking into the sun.

I mug back reassurance on a face
he is still recognising as he turns
away, rampant to a rhythm of rising turf.

Like us, this place is a composite structure,
added to and altered over time;
its archaeology, then, is complex.

The signposts dole out the mysteries
but cannot yield a single isotope
of truth beyond form or dimension.

At the top, he turns once more to face me,
triumphant; his rampart stands him higher,
his head warm under the hat I gifted him.

Maths

The
stupid sums
that men
do.

Conquering Alexander
cut his swathe through
central Asia
to be
shahanshah
and dead,
one month shy
of thirty-three.

Symmetrically,
the Jesus number
accrued a gospel of love
did his stuff,
got nailed
on Friday
and came back
in three.

Geometrically
opposed to me,
my father:
at fifty-eight my
double in years
when he croaked
one day short
of my twenty-ninth.

And now you:
the little Euclid
in my heart,
ticking
ticking off
the fatherless days
as I kiss your mother
and take you to school.

The
stupid sums
that men
do.

Seaton Carew, 1979

I once was a prize bingo wage slave
marking your card for six bob an hour.
Evening stints on the mic, doing it right,

white trash m.c. toastin' rhymes, any line
or four corners. Mates said my voice was pure
Shelley but, never mind the Buzzcocks,

this was business: Kelly's eye, Maggie's den,
baker's dozen, two fat ladies, lucky seven.
When I wasn't calling or checking boards,

I was painting manky outside walls
to *Heart of Glass* from the waltzers next-door.
Soon turned out to be a pain in the ass

so I asked to have back the microphone.
To be alone in the box shelling ping-pongs
from their plastic pod; saving their random

skins from the angry swarm of compressed air.
You were living just a mile up the prom,
Mam far from happy to see me your man.

Bingo called, don't move your markers,
hands off my daughter, wait for the check.

Modern Apprenticeship

He sits on his haunches in the lee of a wall
beneath the scaffold that shelters him from the rain.
Brooks' boy: hoody, baseball cap, *i*-Pod and boots.
Kanye West blows away the morning cobwebs
while the boss is up top with the bag of knives.

Down where the road swings left below the Church,
they have unbundled my first autumn in the village
as the lad learns his trade to some banging bass.
Each leaving, a new stook to unroll the day,
each evening stitched up into moon-bright thatch,

My last view is of silhouette, a straw man
astride the gable, cellphone-quickened
to take a call while Brooks kneels to the sheaves.
I reach the main-road junction to turn right,
as the roof's ribcage barrels behind me:

culm tight, bound against the elements.

Lyneham

The tribal regions fly home tonight;
charred, tagged and flag-draped,
roosting noisily in the guts of a C17.

Tomorrow it will be an eight-hearse cargo
with another ten caskets news-managed
into the middle of next week.

Musandam

Musandam this Spring, and it catches me
unawares: you below the waterline, striped
with sunlight, shade and a sudden renewal;
the tidal come and go of your limbs
to the elver rhythm of the first stroke
taught you by your daddy when you were five.
Your legs forcep buoyancy from the waters
of *Khor Ash Sham* as I fill my lungs and dive
once more down to the point of salvage:
this coralline shard of your living moment,
its passing prefigured in the pallor
of your sunken skin, its quickening a flux
of dark anemone upon the pubic bone.
Head above water, all is every day:
you smiling back at me and our good luck,
the *bedu* bond of salt yet in our guts
to cover the three days here and those three
beyond. It is back down there that everything
is reconceived and passion recommenced.
Through the memory-milt of gulf water
I am brought up short and see
anew the dhow-curve of your middle;
the pelvis set back, like an African girl's,
the buttocks high and compact. Your circling
arms conduct an elegant stop-frame switch
of direction, clear of the island reef.
I surface again and take in the vista:
Musandam's broken fist of limestone
shaken forever at Persia. This was
a pearl coast. Exfoliate but fifty years
from the oil-greased palm of Arabia
and you have the calloused hands

of oarsmen, pulling out to the beds to plunge
long and deep beyond the mortal breath
into zones such as this; redeeming
iridescence from the oyster dark.
With this as my blade, I dive once more
to prise the unworded hinge of moments
such as these: you below the waterline,
in concrete time, reflecting your own light.

Holy Mountain

The sole pilgrim to disembark this morning,
you are met at the dock by a tired young man
and left for hours in the visitor's room.

Later, there'll be a balcony high above
the Aegean, the ferry's come-and-go
and, somewhere out there, a lost Persian fleet.

There will be an unfamiliar liturgy,
strange polyphony in Julian time,
tacit acts of permission and surrender

to the subtle codes of Byzantium.
There will be lukewarm soup, bitter wine
and stale bread; Athonite afterthoughts

of sustenance before the gaze of God.
But, for now, there is the suck-and-pull
of the sea on the rocks below, bidding

you patience. And the jet glint of *ikon*
in the eye of a swallow as she builds
her nest in the monastery walls.

Easter Sunday, Pyrgos

In the time it takes the vapour trail to map
one thousand miles of Greece
                        I have turned
the diminished atlas
of a single page.
                              Above me,
in some terrace café, a meal scatters
voices upon the Aegean;
the click and drang of metal-on-china
                  punctuating the lazy syntax
of the afternoon.

April sun
          drops its lemon juice of chipped light
onto the water,
from left
                       to right,
squeezing out the day's last tang
               over Ammolianí.
We bask beneath this Epitaphion of place;
the here-and-now of camomile,
        the savour of sweet bread
and spit-roast kid.

Christos anesti ek ekron thanato thanaton patissas.

Marinella's

I am told that Neopolitans like a sure thing;
which draws a crowd to line this pavement
in the Christmas Eve sunshine. We take our
macchiati and play guessing games: talent
show hopefuls, celebrity PA, local station
TV news, legendary pastries or the queue
to kiss some godfather's ring. Stripped down
to your sun-vest, you lean forward and whisper
"*Camorra*" then dodge the hit from Capri's
sleepy crocodile out in the bay. The scrimmage
gets testy. Security step in to marshal the fur
and pin-sharp suits, jostling and pushing for
what sure thing? We order more coffee and try
again: soup kitchen, sex show, saint's bones,
Padre Pio, pop star, porn queen, handmade pottery,
de-frocked bishop or the fat boy lottery.
None quite seem to fit the bill, none quite seem
to explain here the random Beatlemania
outside a narrow shop front on *Piazza Vittoria*.
In thirty minute's time, your sister will
meet us from work and put us out of our
misery – silk ties of all things – but now
the molecular press of muster vibrates
to its own traditions and we are joined
for coffee. Eugenio taught his grandson well
about finessing clientele and so Maurizio's
innovation: *sfogliatelle* and espressos
dabbed down the line with the brio of free things,
consumed with the gusto of a public holiday.
I look towards Egg Castle, where the city's crux
lies swaddled against the due of its own breaking:
the way they do things here, the way it's explained.

*Note: Neopolitan legend has it that Castell 'Ovo houses a magic egg which
determines the fate of the whole city; as long as it remains intact.*

Maulds Meaburn

Darkly, down its burrow of Whitsun-past,
a sett stirs in the half-forgotten gloom.

Memory's terrier yapping at your heels,
you sink your trench through hinterland layers

down to the squelching gleys of a childhood.
Maulds Meaburn's shop crosses the beck bridge,

pulling up outside the cramped holiday let.
Three times a week on the passenger seat,

the shopkeeper's pet badger, Rollo:
a rogue exclamation mark, choked-back, leashed.

Butter, milk, eggs and bread distract the
adults, while you take your place at the court

of King Brock; to do his black-and-white
bidding alongside the village children.

Greta

Your favourite sky
        was always to be found
        in lieu of
home: a mother's milk

born of your father;
        his love affair with
           the night and
that sense of lost roads.

Geology

Love becomes a layered thing; its strata
whorled around hours like these.
We are here in some Cornish cove, the ghost
of granite's hot breath upon sandstone scarp
caught, like me, in the act of metamorphosis:
turning now's lamina into the crystalline
glint of mica schist; my shoe the sandglass
tilting this day toward its horizon.

I watch you and the boy pack up and climb
the hill from the beach back to your car;
leaving me to walk the coastal path alone.
In my mind, the moment's fossil: this tiny
span of us, petrified within jurassic time,
laid upon the quick heart's aggregate.

Switchover

Here, news and weather are sung in rounds
while time's a syncopated bleep upon the hour.
You at your mirror and me grinding beans;
each of us, in our own time, tuning in.
Conversation through walls and open doors,
there are echoes, repeats and the hanging
phrase of easily suffered intimacy.
I fail to catch those last two things you said.
Together in here there is clarity:
the bloodless diamond of digital form.
But together in there, in there our wave's
unbroken, obscure and analogue-warm:
we dial the interference of fingers,
pick up the crackling static of kisses.

Visitors Book

Up to Howarth for the early spring –
as was our brief custom – to see
the snowdrops pester out the winter grief
of the Parsonage and retrace songlines
in the slab-bleak churchyard. Half-starved,
you'd drawn all this in, drinking
greedily an unworded recognition,
with the thirst of the thwarted, the held-back
and terraced; like the time in *El Prado*
when I found you weeping before Goya
unable to say why. I pay my fiver
and go inside. A circus family, really,
in their freakishness; with their tiny
feet and tiny books. A puff of wind
could blow them down permanently
and did. You said you felt at home
here, though you couldn't say how.
On a table in the hallway, I see it now
and cannot resist the urge of recollection,
leafing back through the neutral years
until, sure enough, there they are
witnessed by a motley decade
of subsequent strangers: our signatures
in the Visitors Book. The giddy roll
of my stomach at seeing your hand
once more, the blinking out of reason
then the slow, haunted smile to a spring-melt
of memory. 'MM' and 'MM': the rapid
pulse of a small creature short of breath.
You told me on the night of our first
coupling that I'd be pushed away and
you were as good as your word.

Later, in the guesthouse, the landlord
leads me to the same Room 7,
the chipper undertaker of blind ironies.
Our ghosts, aroused, turn to greet me:
a naked threesome splayed and open,
lashed to the bed of non-linear time
in the room where you were last joyful,
in the space where last we were beautiful.

Retiro

A single moment that made worthwhile
the struggle of us. Beside the statue
of Lucifer in the flush July sun:

bright upon your pedestal; swigging
cervezas and bluffing Spanish
while he hennaed *naiads*

onto your arm. I bought you turquoise
and called you beautiful because you were.
And, there in the sunlight, against all your

thirty years, you saw it too. That summer
they'd drained the lake; dredging the dregs,
sediment and jetsam of three decades,

and the corpse of a new-born, cauled in mud,
down among the plastic bags: the saturnine
atrocity of secret black painting.

By the time we strolled *Gran Via* you
had darkened; by the time we reached *Barajas*
a shower had smudged the mermaids.

For Thine is the Kingdom...

In a lock and key-free universe
this is tomcat annihilation.
Barney paws hard at the glass
of the patio doors of your house,
trying to shred the sky-blue silk
beyond. A desperate workout
on the brain's speedball, but I know
where his tabby mind is coming from
if not where it's not going to.
He stares across the free vacuum
of space toward his disproved god,
a man stood helpless in a garden.
I nurse my own cooling star awhile,
write a note, despair of myself and leave.

An Avatar

There, in leftovers upon the white bonnet
of some stranger's car, our moment of high spirits

recycled into monkey god. A *Citroen*
Hanumen: haricot hair, mussel-shell

teeth and melon-skin lips; all picked,
with a drunk's creativity, from the skeleton

of our supper. Dried bread and bottle tops serve
as eyes that gaze sightlessly back at the stars

above Rue Carnot; an Easter Island
challenge to the wit of Madame Côt,

as she bustles past on her way to Mass,
crossing herself and wondering what

manner of heathen prays behind the door
to the avatars of Number Twenty-Four.

Mic-ing the Kit

"Here space is everything, for time ceases to quicken memory."
- Gaston Bachelard

My favourite hour of any session was
mic-ing the kit. Beyer, Electrovoice,
Neumann, Sennhauser, AKG and Shure;
sensitive diaphragms, phantom power.

This was analogue, unsampled and raw,
the real business of capturing sound:
the cottage loaf of pressure gradients,
the sideways heart of cardioid response.

Often, I would send away the drummer,
ply him with tea or weed to leave me there
- free of his twitches and random hits -
alone with his kit, sexing it in space.

There were the routine no-brainers, holy
trinities and givens: bass drum, hi-hat
and snare meant the egg of the D-twelve,
C-four-one-four, SM fifty-seven.

There was the metalwork and toms, beloved
of drummers disliked by myself. Always
I did my best by them: stringing up condensers,
top mic-ing the mounted mids, crash and ride.

Then things got interesting in the room
with your own little signatures or tricks.
A woodcutter now, you knew the grain
of the space; its sweet spots and hard-knots.

The snare's true *logos* was to be had reflected
from some wall or favourite corner; it's kingfisher
reverb caught fire in a Gents' urinal,
where the porcelain gave sympathetic decay.

Making my way back to the control room
through the vineyard of leads, through the heavy
anechoic doors, I was usually happy.
Artisan's work: preparing the dance.

Haas Effect

For John Martyn

Between 30 and 40 milliseconds,
the human ear incorporates sounds
arriving from two separate sources;
letting time drift beyond that duration
before perceiving them as distinct:
that's as *delay* (audio effect) or,
in common terms, *echo* (phenomenon).
Observing this law of the first wave front
is an involuntary sensory inhibition
mirrored in your memory;
the acoustics of which can be cruel.

So, a new amputee is tortured by
the invisible itch and reaches down
to scratch solid air, before advancing
toward his future on an unsteady leg;
and I am awake before dawn, hearing
a voice and embracing space, with you
already two hours away; effecting
your own precedence in the fast lane.
A motorway's flattened grey wave
of white noise and forgetting...

Decades

I'm driving my mother
through Connemara; on the shortest day
of the year. Lenaun, Kylemore,
Cashel, Cong, Maam Cross, Letterfrack:
the names slipping sequentially
through the gloom, a rosary
of sung syllables through the knuckled
hours. Stone field, bog, lough, rock, bay,
swan, lough, bog, bay, field, stone.
It's her seventieth birthday.
Glory be to the Father,
and to the Son and to the Holy
Spirit and to something else
I can't quite name: a memory
maybe, a nurtured reflex or ghost
of the small boy that walks me yet.
Hauling me down to Stations
or Benediction, we bonded
through the resentment of missed
Blake's Seven and mumbled decades.
My tribal drum was the rhythm
of words and words repeated;
phrases circling back upon them-
selves, like country lanes leading
to unclear crossroads. Snapping
to at the memory bell, I am summoned
to this newer communion
with the drunken crow of Ireland's roads.

It is getting late. In my rear-view
the solstice sun thins out

against the wild Atlantic as
before me, black and huge, *Croagh Patrick*
mars the horizon with the dark
obligation of an evening
Mass from a Sunday teatime long
ago. Greater still, my mother
in the passenger seat; the decades
dropping from her sleeping face
till she's the girl emerging
from *John Collier's* factory gates
into my father's embrace.
I am stumbling around
in the back seat of our clapped-out A40;
trying to get a better view, sniffing
a moment with the gusto of my
full four-and-three-quarter years.

Later, at a smart restaurant
back in Westport,
it is she who will stumble;
words eluding
her in the stress of what
she thinks is expected of her. Sure
before her God, she wavers
before the cutlery. The chef's
questions demanding the response
of an unfamiliar creed.
In a gesture learnt
from her, I reach out
across the space, hand enfolding hand,
fingers guiding fingers
to the right prayer; grasp,
at last, upon the right bead.

Digitalis

Between his first and third heart attack
passed my father's Summer of Love.
An unknown younger man came back:

my ear-ring was no longer mocked
- nor the tattoo of an arrowed dove -
between his first and third heart attack.

A sudden awareness of hip-hop and rap
a shuffling of beat groups with dub;
as an unknown younger man came back.

I'd come across him trying on hats
and found him once weeping at foxgloves
between his first and third heart attack.

Aware that given time is not given back,
he started bending lifelong rules enough
to let me see the younger man come back.

Dad was Dylan, McCartney and Jack Kerouac
in that last fond Summer of Love;
between his first and third heart attack
when an unknown younger man came back.

Phoenix

It went within a month of the funeral:
the old Parkray with its cracked-glass grin.
Ma never got the knack of it, so he'd
set about making plans for the legacy
of a 'living flame'; laying off the odd yankee
double and trixie to cover his tracks.
To this day, Aunt Norah gets her Widow's Coal
while my mother remains suspicious
of the naked spark, like a spooked hen
with a fox at the wire. But the old man
bent to it with indulgence, as to a
favourite terrier; coaxing its stubborn
streak to loyalty and tricks of warmth.
Now, years off, this small rite of remembrance:
Ma standing back, me on my knees – as
the sudden gasp of air into newspaper lung
draws the cavity's ghost into flame.

Echoes

Every Saturday morning I'd come down
to see a tight brown roll-up hanging
from the puckered flap of the letterbox.

Awaiting Dad – in lieu of salt fish – was
Grandma's proxy of one twelfth motherlove:
news from home, the week's Liverpool Echoes.

With her old man lost at sea, she'd 'seen' Richard
wave to her from the parlour on the very
morning he'd stopped a bullet in Normandy

and buried Betty after that bomb destroyed
the munitions factory. With Jimmy now
a Bevan Boy and her old man back but lairy,

she guarded the survivors jealously.
National Service had taken Our Alec
to Catterick and, demobbed, thence to West

Hartlepool via the Rink Ballroom and
my mother. The seventh son, he needed
some looking after and the Fifties *Mappa*

Mundi read, 'There be monsters' somewhere east
of Leeds. Lob Scouse didn't post and supply lines
were being stretched; hence this sphere of influence

demarcated by string and brown paper,
scrolled around the throttled daily tidings
that would gather at home through the day shift.

Now posted exotica exciting a grandchild,
love's woodbine would poke, without fail,
from the docker's gob at the foot of our stairs.

Liverpool-Irish

My father endured the taunts of 'tick'
(from a man called Keenan) and bore
the nickname 'Paddy' uneasily;
yet would stiffen to the reel
and set his jaw for the camera.

He would laugh at the Pier Head Irish,
gazing out beyond the river's foggy mouth
to a neglectful motherland, through eyes
distant in drink and false memory;
doing the math on the rounds and neatly

balancing their cost against that to re-buy
the family farm. Yet he was in clover
to hear his name in *The Irish Rover*
and talked of cousins in Wicklow
with the requisite exile's glow.

This celtic *mestizo* thing is awkward.
Fit to be called diaspora, commodified
in song, yet welcome back but slowly,
when we've stayed away too long: history's
tenant cousins twice-removed.

I was once suspect enough for passport
stamps, *MON DROIT* and my name to keep me
all day in Holyhead for routine questions.
but my accent's enough still to Cromwell our pitch
in some *gaeltacht* pub in Ballynahinch.

Cathal

He lived below me at the Rusholme flat
and pronounced my name in the Irish,
putting *air* into the squat Anglo-Saxon
of the first syllable; filling the house,
most days, with the ripe breath of boiled cabbage.

He could have been anything from fifty-five
to seventy, surely too old to be leaving
the muddy lanes of Monaghan for the
Manchester rain. Then again, he might
have been in that bedsit years before I

passed through. The house was doused
in his tenancy, wore his stain on its
fingers, like porter and nicotine.
I would clock him on the stairs, shrinking
back into the shadows of shy custom.

We shared a stout and chaser in the snug
of *O'Neil's* one mizzling Monday teatime;
he telling me about yer man in Flat 3
and the landless, collarless inheritance
of the middle sons of rural south Ulster.

Exactly *what* he did, to keep himself
in Guinness and fags, I never did find out.
What I do know is this: when they forced
the front door, he was in the hall. They said
I was their brother, so aside he stood.

Anything for a quiet life, he slipped
back to the Sacred Heart and his gas stove,

– an angelus, baccy and boiled bacon –
while my new siblings made hay with the stuff;
bringing in my harvest of fence-able goods.

Their exit was a poacher's hook, torn from
salmon flesh. Back downstairs they called on
Cathal: a rosary of broken teeth,
a Shannon of blood, Kennedy's Dallas head.
A sister took him in, is what I heard.

Home International

Father Eamon took the team talk:
"Brendan get out and score a hat-trick
or you're gonna end up in purgatory
with the souls of un-baptised babies."
No pressure then. This was back when
we were ten and a bloodied Bogside
was in sore need of a holiday. Sorry
for their troubles, the church shipped them
over. Fifteen lads from Belfast and Derry
billeted around the good catholic families.

The local rag ran a picture and story;
I have it yet before me: all smiles, handshakes
and kick-off by some visiting missionary.
In borrowed boots and Doc Martens, high-waisters
flapping at half mast, they did their best
but Jesus Christ was a Hartlepudlian
and we were on home turf. With Kelly in goal,
defence of Murphy, the Lineghans and Malone,
midfield of Robertson, Farrell and Waller,
and, upfront, Brendan Christie walked on water.

No player, wee Michael took to lobbing grenades
or taking aim at some distant patrol
as our winger waltzed by him. Big Fergus
preferred my father's milk float, its click and whirr,
to this particular game of soldiers.
The score totted up to a baker's dozen.
Took me ten years to work out why was chinned
the wag who quipped *Parish thirteen Paddies nil*.
A classy finisher, Brendan bagged his trinity:
goals netting souls out in Eamon's limbo.

Seven Views of Christopher

I
Tub-faced boy, rocking
back and forth and back. Both hands
flapping: flightless bird.

II
Always at thresholds
friend of doors; their completion
his fascination.

III
Tick-tock walk with feet
at ten-to-two; another
obsession is time.

IV
Fire drill, downpour, not
best pleased, saved by Christopher
class surrealist.

V
No blue-eye contact,
focused-in: peripheral
Buddha of himself.

VI
Bad weekend, I hear:
Police called in. Growing boy
strikes shrinking father.

VII
Annual Review,
concern all round. Explaining:
this is who he is.

Afters

Lying in bed
               sleepily
reading Kavanagh
               and talking philosophy.
something said
               about your grandmother
having been
               the queer fella's
sometime sweetheart,
               burrs me with
a spectral sadness:
               at what is lost
and what merely past.
               A fine distinction;
like memories
               of De Valera's
monochrome Eire,
               when the piebald
collar held sway
               and the second man
ever to hold you
               on that Monaghan
February day
               was the self-same
cropper poet.
               Blinking, in the late
night upstairs room,
               at the newborn
I now hold under
               an altogether
different gaze.

Sufficient

what did for him
was actually a fragment
of bone from her *humerus*;

the same right arm
that would finish him off
when they fucked

without this shard of lover's ivory
– ripping into his face
for the money shot of death –

he might have survived the blast
that tore through the bus, reducing her
to blood vapour and body matter

finally they identified her
by the rough scintilla
which did for him

24 Rue Carnot

This house lolls in a droiling back street.
The army-issue blanket of working week sleep
is rolled aside for a thousand-egg omelette
flipping dreams of fish and strange meetings.

In this bed I drive to Lagrasse to chat
to a long dead friend in some doorway;
him blue-eyed and smiling, while the mistral
shifts the dust around our unshod toes.

The early bell of St. Maurice tickles slumber
in the slow flow of morning hours, teases
my waking with the hyper-real: a stream
of lost lovers slides across my stomach.

The velux rasp of rain on a roof window
lowers the room's lid and drives me back to this:
a child's rest again, our tangle of limbs,
these dreams and, on a clear night, your star.

Taxi Fares

. . . .were a delicate matter, even when
you skipped up the steps in your long,
long leather coat, courting abandon
dressed as sex, freedom, passion and ease,
or, rather, what you guessed I sought in these.

What the shattered circuitry of your past
could not detect were the slow, sad pulses
of insight from my own; x-raying beyond
the leather, thong and pink décolletage
to our remembrance day walk through Richmond.

Skipping the Carnival, we go looking
for closure, ten years after the man
with my forename had offered a bed,
some place to sleep off the student party.
That bright young you yessed like a convent girl.

When he'd finished, he hauled you down
the stairs into the dawn, hailed a hackney
and flung you in with a covering twenty:
a quid for each year. Which is why I stay
indoors and never offer, while you pay.

Remembering Helen

Like all Troys, mine was never meant to end
happily. *Estranged* is a galley that floats
upon a broad ocean of possibility.
Ringless, you washed up on the shore of me;
keen and gorgeous, unfathomed by your men,
draped in the bladderwrack of discontent,
bearing gifts from the sea: salty harvest,
secret pearls and a riptide of desire.

When Menalaus found that old e-mail,
I looked him cold in the eye and asked
if we were talking or fighting; then saw
what he needed: the lie, mythology
renewed, a more convenient proof.
And so I lied, my love, I lied for him,
your sons and you; forgetting that lovers
– even mothers – want only their love's truth.

So, the ships stayed at home and you moved
into your brother's. The city was saved awhile,
for the sake of the kids and you got some space.
We would meet from time to time, unable
to unlearn the story nor take it forward;
I moved north to make or break its thread
and you forgot your lines. Now, for the last time,
I am giving you back, giving you back to the sea.

33 Birchtree Road

The smell of you hung on awhile longer:
sheets, pillows and towel scented by skin.
Weird and compelling its force;
stinking with the it of things,
like the old man's favourite sweater
one week after we buried him.
The wet hairs you brushed out with
comic aside will dance in the draught
by the kitchen door, or catch the static
moment of opportunity to remind me.

Evensong

The town is cashing-up as you arrive, glimpsed
through windows shutting shop on the day.
Low sky and March rain opaque over Sarum,
you drive against the storm-drain flow of cars
quitting the centre for home. With a sick note's
gift of time, park up and stroll the streets
towards the spire. Exchanging drizzle
for gloom, you pause; adjust faculties
to incense, gold and blue-refracted light.
A warden robins forward, all tact, hymnal
and subtle appraisal: *Opus Anglicanum.*
The blind habits of a childhood creed
have you genuflect and cross yourself,
dropping to a quick Hail Mary, before
sitting to absorb this vaulted space,
new to the threshing-floor of memory.
In daffodil shawl and John Lennon cap
a woman makes ostentatious her late arrival,
comfortable in the habit of attendance.
It is the Annunciation. Talk is of a girl,
an angel and word-made-flesh: *Fra Angelica's*
moment rendered flat to time, in pink and blue.
And how substance can be lost amid a flutter
of wings; beaten back by physics, doubt and
carbon dating. The *Kyrie* rises beyond
logic, perching upon a pinhead of air,
before diminishing down its span of reverb:
this nightingale-wood of perceivable sound.
A sudden itch between the shoulder blades
and glance at your watch tell you it is
time to leave. Outside, a blackbird laces
the twilight with its uneven song. You walk
through the precincts, back towards the city;
clipped and flightless, a messenger of sorts.

Epithalamion for the Groom

On the marriage of Sharon Gleave and Alexander Kirichenko

It becomes about lists: guests, songs,
places, blooms and invitations,
though our angels enumerate
the truer manifest: you, me, us.

It revolves around errands: cars,
priest, tailor, florist, caterer.
While my job-weary heart labours;
seeking its orbit around you.

I am sent to the shop, pacing
out yards in years spent together;
counting outward a history
and returning through our future.

Alone on the doorstep, outside
the kitchen window, I listen
to the voices of you with your
sisters and smile at the plotting.

This moment I shall hold with me
fast as a child holds Christmas Eve;
eyes tight, deep with the winter-turn.
And tomorrow I will wed thee.

I go inside to more lists: food,
friends, music, wine and family.
No longer does it trouble me, for my
heart's inventory is full of you.

Merula

Since five this rest has been the rightful due
of the blackbird; my sleep refashioned
upon the filigree anvil of his song.

The cherry tree, clover patch and yew,
the wall, my slumber and the lattice gate
are his dominion: a feudal estate.

The black *signeur*, still singing
from here through Petrarch and yet back,
pays his dues to older gods.

That Last Defence

I wake up with blood in my mouth
and a dream of percussion, my wife
hushing me back to the canvas
upon which I've been painted by
the unseen hook he slipped past my
guard. Twenty years of blood-metal
tang and flashback, that concussion
stitched now and morphine-morphed into
sleep: the bed wet with punches, sweat
and viscera. The doctors are busy,
counting, counting, counting me out,
while the papers file their copy
ready for an ex-champ's obituary:
King of the Ring fights on to the bell.

It comes to us all: the one last purse,
that last defence. The challenger,
younger and always hungrier,
wrapping his hands, lacing the gloves
that knock you cold then drive the hearse.
This cancer, gnawing at the bone-ghost
of my today, joined my corner that night.
Whisper it above the cornered
conversation, the tears and lesions;
this is the sweet science of champions.
Death lands with the first K.O.,
the blow that strips away the belt,
that travels down from jaw to toes,
fusing the lights on your Vegas Strip.

Best Kite on the Hill

Back at Uffington, the line heavier now
with a history; its haul weighty
beyond the burden of ground hefty
with its own tales. You, me and your son
and the best kite on the hill.
Passing around the string, sharing the pull
of possibility, we are shaken;
shuddering through the kite-tail spine
of ourselves, alone in the moment's blue
latitude. I look from boy to you
with a sense of new gravities.
An inkling load guyed skyward, upon
the caught breath of an idea murmured
into your ear: you, me, us. The boy turns
away, hood hoisted against the breeze;
lost to the glider's warp: Epona's
child yet. His soul at anchor there,
dragging the pale kedge of nine year-old
shoulder, quickens at its easy primacy;
steady in the heaven of his summer.
The foregone chronicles of a million
ghosts haunt the vaulted arc of air
that drags at the bellied line. Yet, whilst
others struggle to cheat the pull of
primeval earth, the white horse favours
him with the lift of new stories;
silently mouthed to himself alone,
rapt in the kite's thrumming NOW.
Shall we not figure in these fables?
Up there, do we find our correlative?
Or, loaded with history, circumstance
and doubt, do we quiver, veer and fall?
Shot falcons, ploughing ourselves
back into the waiting hillside.